Amazing Bears

EYEWITNESS JUNIORS

Amazing
Bears

WRITTEN BY
THERESA GREENAWAY

PHOTOGRAPHED BY
DAVE KING

ALFRED A. KNOPF • NEW YORK

Conceived and produced by
Dorling Kindersley Limited

Project editor Louise Pritchard
Art editor Hans Verkroost
Managing editor Sophie Mitchell
Managing art editor Miranda Kennedy
Production Shelagh Gibson

Illustrations by Ruth Lindsay, Dan Wright, and Julie Anderson
Bears supplied by Clubb-Chipperfield Ltd (pp 10/11, 18/19, 22/23);
Natura Artis Magistra, Amsterdam (pp 20/21); Parc Zoologique de Paris (pp 8/9,
12/13, 14/15, 16/17, 24/25, 28/29); Whipsnade Zoo (pp 26/27);
Editorial consultant Daphne Hills
Special thanks to Ray Moller for photography pp 26/27; Mike Dunning for photography pp 20/21;
Laurence Paoli and Nicole Morse for their help in supplying bears for photography;
David Fung and Carl Gombrich for research

This is a Borzoi Book published by Alfred A. Knopf, Inc.

First American edition, 1992

Manufactured in Italy 0 9 8 7 6 5 4 3 2 1

Library of Congress Cataloging in Publication Data
Greenaway, Theresa.
Amazing bears / written by Theresa Greenaway;
photographed by Dave King.
p. cm. – (Eyewitness Juniors; 23)
Includes index.
Summary: Introduces the physical characteristics and
habits of bears and pandas.
1. Bears – Juvenile literature. 2. Pandas – Juvenile
literature. [1. Bears.
2. Pandas.] I. King, Dave, ill.
II. Title. III. Series.
QL737.C27G739 1992 599.74'446–dc20 92–910
ISBN 0-679-82769-2
ISBN 0-679-92769-7 (lib. bdg.)

Color reproduction by Colourscan, Singapore
Printed in Italy by A. Mondadori Editore, Verona

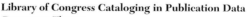

Contents

*These children are about
4 ft tall. They will show
you how big the bears are.*

What is a bear?

They may look cuddly, but bears lose their temper quickly and can be dangerous. So remember – if you want to cuddle a bear, make sure it's your friendly teddy!

Chompers
Powerful jaws and teeth allow bears to eat lots of different food – tough stems and roots, lumps of meat, and hard nuts, as well as fruit and leaves.

Useful paws
Bears have five toes – and five claws – on each foot. Bears use their front paws for many jobs, such as catching and holding prey, digging for insects and roots, and, of course, climbing trees.

Splash!
This European brown bear is enjoying itself! All bears can swim, and they are quite happy in water, where they can catch fish or cool off on a hot day.

Sma
roun
ear

Thi
fur

Meet the family

Bears and pandas are mammals. There are seven kinds of bears and two kinds of pandas. These koalas (left) are not bears. They are marsupials – mammals that have a pouch in front in which they carry their babies when they are small.

Caring mother

At three or four months old, bear cubs are ready to go into the outside world. Like all bears, this black bear cub will stay with Mom until it is about two years old and can look after itself.

Fast growers

Newborn bears like this brown bear cub are kept safe inside a den. At first the cubs are tiny and helpless. Their eyes are closed and they cannot walk. But they grow quickly on the rich, fatty milk from their mother.

On two feet

Like humans, bears walk flat on the soles of their feet. This makes it easy for them to stand up on their hind legs. They often do this to have a good look around, to threaten an enemy, or just to reach for something.

Supersense

Bears use their senses to help them survive. They have good hearing and a strong sense of smell. Although people used to believe bears had poor eyesight, it is now thought that they can see perfectly well.

American black bear

The black bear is North America's most common bear. There may be as many as 750,000 black bears living in Canada, the USA, and Mexico.

Going to town
Although they are usually shy creatures, some black bears have grown very used to humans. It is no surprise in some towns to see a bear padding along the street.

Bear's picnic
Bears have found out that visitors to national parks bring picnics. One bear learned that if he jumped up and down on top of a certain kind of car, the doors burst open and he could then get into the car and eat all the food!

Coat of many colors
Most black bears are, of course, black. But there are also brown, beige, cinnamon, white, and blue black bears. This rare cream-colored black bear is called a Kermode's bear.

Survival experts
Black bears are intelligent animals and can survive in a range of places. Most live in forests and woods, but some live by the sea, in the mountains, and even in swamps.

Favorite toy
Teddy bears were first known as Teddy's bears, named for President Theodore Roosevelt. They became popular after Roosevelt refused to shoot a young black bear in 1902.

Black bears have small eyes and round ears

Not fussy

Leaves, nuts, berries, roots, and fruit make up most of a black bear's diet. But the bear will eat almost anything it can get its paws on, including insects and small mammals – and, of course, honey!

Tree climber

Black bears can run at 30 miles an hour if they have to, but when frightened they usually climb a tree. Cubs are very good at climbing too and often find safety in the branches of a tree.

orter claws han those of most ther bears

Sun bear

Also called the Malayan and the honey bear, this is the smallest of all bears. It lives in the tropical forests of Southeast Asia, which are hot year-round.

Bowlegged bear
The sun bear is a good tree climber and spends more time in trees than any other bear. Its bow-legs make it look awkward when it is walking, but it can move very fast.

Rare bear
Because they are in danger of extinction, sun bears are protected in some countries. As more and more forest is cut down, the bears have less space in which to live and find food.

Short black fur

Out of its skin
A sun bear has very loose skin. If it is grabbed by a large animal it can wriggle its body far enough to turn around and bite its attacker!

Sunrise
Sun bears get their name from the yellowish mark on their chest, which is thought to look like the rising sun. But some sun bears have plain black chests.

Sunbathing
During the day sun bears like to doze in a tree. They sometimes make themselves comfortable on a nest of branches that they build in the treetops.

Midnight feast
All through the night this hard-working bear searches for all sorts of tasty tidbits – small animals, lizards, insects, fruit, and leaves. Using its strong claws, it scratches under logs, climbs up trees, and even digs into tree trunks to get at sticky honeycombs.

Paler-colored nose

Long claws and hairless soles of the feet for gripping branches

Tongue twister
The tongue of a sun bear is extremely long. When the bear has dug out a nest of juicy termites, it allows the insects to run over its paws and then licks them off with its tongue.

Polar bear

The frozen sea around the North Pole is polar bear country. The bears live at the sea's edge, traveling south in winter as the ice spreads and north in spring as it melts.

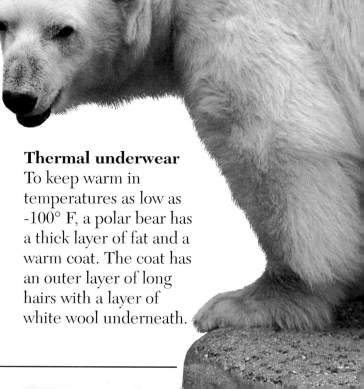

Junk food
Polar bears can only hunt for seals and fish from sea ice. So in summer, when the ice melts, the bears start searching for food in garbage dumps.

Patient hunter
A big bear has to eat one seal every 11 days. It will sit for hours by a seal's breathing hole in the ice, waiting for the seal to come up for air. Then it will spring forward and kill the seal.

A polar bear's nose and tongue are black, as is the rest of its skin

Varied diet
Polar bears eat more meat than other bears. They will kill seabirds, fish, crabs, and seals. And they are happy to scavenge on a dead whale if they come across one in their travels.

Thermal underwear
To keep warm in temperatures as low as -100° F, a polar bear has a thick layer of fat and a warm coat. The coat has an outer layer of long hairs with a layer of white wool underneath.

owed in

uring a blizzard, a polar bear
rls up with its back to the wind
d sleeps until the storm passes.
doesn't mind – too much – if it
s covered with snow!

Ice den

In autumn, pregnant
female polar bears dig a den in
the snow and give birth to their cubs,
usually twins, in the winter. In spring, the cubs
go with Mom on short trips away from the den.

Polar paddler

Polar bears have strong, partially
webbed front paws. They are
excellent swimmers and can stay
underwater for
two minutes.

*White fur helps
the polar bear to
hide in the snow*

Spectacled bear

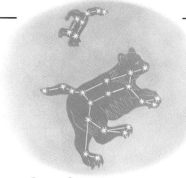

This bear has a shorter muzzle, or snout, than other bears. A long time ago, several kinds of short-muzzled bears roamed all over North and South America. Now the spectacled bear is the only one left.

Hello up there!
You can see bears in the sky – but they are not wearing spectacles! The are the two constellations called the Great Bear and the Little Bear.

Eye marks
The pale fur around the eyes gives this bear its name. The "spectacles" come in lots of styles, and often spread into a "bib" on the chest.

A bear in the paw
Young bears need the protection of their mother until they are big enough to defend themselves. Sometimes a mother spectacled bear holds her cub against her body with one paw while running along – on three legs.

No humans allowed
Spectacled bears are shy and stay as far away from humans as possible. They have short legs, which means they can travel through thick parts of the forest where humans cannot go.

Up a tree
Much of a spectacled bear's time
is spent in trees, sleeping and eating.
In fact, these bears sometimes
stay in a tree until all its fruit
has ripened – and been eaten.

"Spectacles"
around
eyes

Lone ranger
The spectacled bear is the only
bear in South America, and
there are probably no more than
2,000 left. These bears used to live
in grassland and semi-desert, but
humans are taking over this land and
forcing the bears away. Now, most are
found in the thick tropical forests of
the northern Andes mountains.

Shaggy
black fur

Brown bear

There are brown bears in Europe, North America, and Asia. These groups have lived apart for thousands of years. Now they are a little bit different from each other.

A brown bear has a huge, wide head and strong jaws

Senior citizen

Brown bears are often called grizzlies in North America. This is because some of them have fur tipped with silvery white, making them look "grizzled," or as if they are going gray.

Gone fishin'

Every summer, when salmon swim upriver, the bears go fishing using claws and teeth. Some bears just snap the fish out of the air as the salmon leap up a waterfall.

Big bear

The Kodiak bear from Kodiak Island in Alaska is the largest brown bear in the world. An adult male can weigh over 1,320 pounds – as much as eight grown men.

Bear hug

Among bears, a hug is not always a friendly action! Young male bears do play together, but this is practice for when they are older and need to fight for territory or females.

Claws are shorter on the back paws than the front paws

The large hump on the shoulders is made of fat and muscle

Food from the forest

Brown bears live in forests, where they eat mostly leaves, berries, and roots. But they will eat insects, rodents, fish, carrion (dead animals), and even young deer.

Winter storage

In winter, in places where it gets very cold, there is not much for bears to eat. Then they dig a den in the ground. They curl up inside and sleep until spring comes – sometimes for as long as seven months.

American-born

This brown bear comes from North America. There are about 50,000 brown bears in North America. Most of them live in Canada and Alaska.

Sloth bear

When Europeans first saw sloth bears they thought that they were related to another mammal called a sloth, so they called them bear sloths. When scientists realized that they were bears, the name was turned around to sloth bear.

Piggyback
Mother sloth bears carry their two or three cubs on their back. The babies cling tightly to the long fur and bury their faces it when they are scared.

Under tigers' protection
The number of sloth bears in the wild is decreasing. But where they are found with the Bengal tiger, their numbers are increasing. This is because the tiger is protected, so the sloth bear gets protection too.

Curved claws up to 3 inches long

Friendly bear
Unlike many bears, sloth bears like some company. Adults can sometimes be seen together resting or searching for food.

Noisy eater
Once they have broken into a termite nest, the bears form their lips into a tube, blow away any dust blocking the hole, then noisily suck out the termites like a vacuum cleaner. The sound can be heard up to 600 feet away!

A nose for ants
A sloth bear's long nose is perfect for eating ants and termites. The nose is not as hairy as the rest of its body, and the bear can close its nostrils so the insects don't crawl up.

lawing their way in
ermites are a tasty treat
r sloth bears. These
sects make huge mud
omes that bake hard in
e sun. The bears dig
to the nests with their
ng, curved claws.

Shaggy fur

Day dreamer
Sloth bears live in the forests of India, Nepal, and Sri Lanka. They rest during the day and are active at night, shuffling around on the forest floor or climbing trees in search of food.

Asiatic black bear

Also known as the Tibetan black bear or the Himalayan black bear, this bear lives in the forests of eastern Asia and Japan. It is at home in cold mountain forests or in warmer lowland forests.

In danger
Asiatic black bears could soon be extinct. People kill them for use in medicines or because they think the bears are dangerous.

Keep away
These bears are well known for their bad temper. There are many stories of people who went too close to a bear and were hurt or killed.

Moon bears
Because of the white crescent on its chest, the Asiatic black bear is often called the moon bear. Its scientific name means "moon bear of Tibet."

Out all hours
Asiatic black bears often hunt for food during the day. But if people live nearby, the bears may hide away during the day and come out at night.

In trouble again
Asiatic black bears scratch and chew the bark off trees. Unfortunately, Japan's most valuable timber trees – cedar and cypress – seem to be their favorite flavors.

Treehouse
In order to reach as many fruits and nuts as possible, Asiatic black bears sit in the treetops and bend the branches toward them. These build up into a kind of nest called an *enza*.

Strong claws are useful when climbing trees

Collar of long fur around the shoulders

Crescent of white fur

Dancing bear
Asiatic black bears can walk on two legs better than any other bear. Sadly, this means that some people catch cubs and train them to perform in circuses.

大熊猫 Giant panda

The bamboo forests of central and western China are home to the giant panda. It is one of the world's rarest animals. There are probably no more than 1,000 left.

Black eyes

A Chinese legend tells why giant pandas are black and white. Long ago they were all white. One day they went to the funeral of a young girl with ashes on their arms as a sign of respect. They were very sad. They wiped their eyes to dry the tears, hugged themselves in sorrow, and covered their ears with their paws to block out the sound of crying. And wherever they touched themselves the ashes stained their fur black.

Bedtime

Giant pandas sleep a lot to save energy. They may make themselves comfortable in a tree or curl up in a bamboo patch and rest their head on a hind leg.

Keeping warm

In winter, the forests are covered in snow. But giant pandas don't mind. Their large, round bodies keep in the heat, and their thick, oily fur coat keeps them warm and dry.

Rock-a-bye, baby

Female pandas are loving mothers. They cradle their tiny cub in their arms almost continuously until it is strong enough to walk.

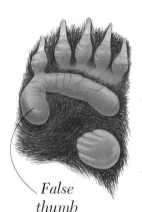

False thumb

Thumbs up

Pandas have five toes and a bony, muscular lump on their front paws, like a false thumb. This helps them to grip bamboo stems.

A panda's black markings do not appear until it is two weeks old

Strong jaws and teeth are needed to chew bamboo

Bamboo binge
Bamboo is a tall, tough kind of grass which makes up most of the pandas' diet. Pandas have to eat 45 pounds of bamboo a day to keep up their strength. And eating takes them about 14 hours!

Red panda

Raccoon

The red panda was the first panda to be called a panda, but nobody knows why. In fact, this panda might be a raccoon – the experts are still arguing about it!

A tail of warmth

Red pandas are about 3 feet long. Almost half of this is their thick tail, which they often use to help them keep warm as they sleep.

Long whiskers for feeling their way in the dark

Food mixer

Like its giant cousin, the red panda eats mostly bamboo and has a false thumb so that it can grasp the plant stems. It also likes fruits, berries, and small birds.

Night prowler

Red pandas live in thick forests on the Himalaya Mountains of western China, Nepal, Assam, and northern Myanmar. They are active at night, searching for food.

Happy families

Female red pandas give birth to a litter of usually two cubs each year. Mother and cubs may stay together until the next litter is due. Then the youngsters go off to lead their own lives.

Red panda cub

Long, ringed tail – similar to a raccoon's tail

Non-slip

The pads on the bottom of a red panda's paws are furry. Together with sharp claws, this helps the pandas to climb trees – especially wet trees – without slipping.

Sun bather

Eating bamboo does not give the pandas a great deal of energy, which they need to keep warm as well as to climb through the trees. So to save energy, the red panda sleeps a lot – if possible, in the sun.

Catlike

Because of its rich red fur, the red panda was called a fire cat when it was first discovered. Just like a cat, it licks a front paw to give its face a good washing, and spits and hisses when it is angry!

Bear talk

All animals have their own ways of talking to each other. A bear must use its ears, eyes, and nose to understand signals from other bears.

Scratching

One way to "talk" to another bear is to leave signs. Male bears scratch marks on trees to tell other bears they are around. And, of course, the higher the scratches the bigger the bear!

The Syrian brown bear is smallest of the brown be...

Body language

Bears use their body to talk. If a bear lowers its head toward you, it is probably about to attack. So never bend down in front of a bear. It will think you are about to attack and may try to get you first.

Don't blink

This Syrian brown bear is not looking at the camera, but that doesn't mean it cannot see the photographer. Bears only stare at each other to show that they are not going to be friendly.

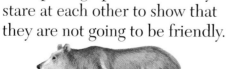

Acrobat

By leaving a message for others to read, bears and pandas avoid unwanted meetings and even fights and injury. They often spray their scent to mark their territory. Giant pandas sometimes do a handstand to leave their scent high on a tree.

isy language

th bears are noisy,
they like to talk to
ch other – by
ring, howling,
ealing, huffing,
tling, and gurgling.

This is mine!

It is often necessary for bears to argue over territory. With their mouths wide open, these two grizzly bears are growling loudly at each other, both trying to win the argument.

Index